Peter Fronteddu and Stefan Steigerwald

Making Integral Knives

Schiffer Publishing Ltd
4880 Lower Valley Road, Atglen, Pennsylvania 19310

Other Schiffer Books By The Author:

Pocketknife Making for Beginners,
978-0-7643-3847-2, $29.99
The Lockback Folding Knife: From Design to Completion,
978-0-7643-3509-9, $29.99

Other Schiffer Books on Related Subjects:

Basic Knifemaking: From Raw Steel to a Finished Stub Tang Knife,
978-0-7643-3508-2, $29.99

Originally published as *Integralmesser: Schritt für Schritt von der Konstruktion zum fertigen Messer* by Wieland Verlag GmbH.
Translated by Dr. Edward Force
Cover design and layout by Caroline Wydeau

Schiffer Publishing Ltd.
4880 Lower Valley Road
Atglen, PA 19310
Phone: (610) 593-1777; Fax: (610) 593-2002
E-mail: Info@schifferbooks.com

In Europe, Schiffer books are distributed by
Bushwood Books
6 Marksbury Ave.
Kew Gardens
Surrey TW9 4JF England
Phone: 44 (0) 20 8392 8585; Fax: 44 (0) 20 8392 9876
E-mail: info@bushwoodbooks.co.uk
Website: www.bushwoodbooks.co.uk

Library of Congress Control Number: 2011943135

Revised Design by Stephanie Daugherty
Type set in Ctourier Std/Frutiger LT Std

ISBN: 978-0-7643-4011-6
Printed in China

CONTENTS

FOREWORD

Making knives is becoming more and more popular as a hobby. Increasingly, people are finding out how pleasurable it is to make a nice and practical object like a knife. There is scarcely another object that can be, and in such a convincing way, a tool, collector's item, aesthetic object, and even a work of art all in one. The knife, as man's oldest companion, holds a very special status in every way.

With this workshop series we want to provide assistance on any and all technical questions and thus help you avoid pitfalls and mistake. This series of books presents a variety of subjects and ways to make knives; it is set up so that you can complete and copy every individual step. Here we have put special emphasis on the practical and workshop use of the books.

Following the volumes *Pocketknife Making for Beginners*, *The Lockback Folding Knife*, and *Basic Knifemaking*, this book is now the fourth volume in the series. Experience gained in compiling the previous books, plus constructive criticism from readers, have contributed to this book.

We have tried to portray every step of the process as understandably as possible. What we cannot do is provide you with a basic introduction to essential handcrafting ability with saws, drills, or files. That would make this book much too large. But if you have never held a hammer in your hand, then it would be best to start by acquiring some basic experience before you venture on your first knife. But have no fear: You do not need to take a course in using tools to be able to practice the knifemaker's hobby with success and pleasure. And when you encounter limits to your equipment or ability, you can always turn to the books in this series.

In any case, you should read the descriptions in this book thoroughly before you start to work. This way you will know what you are facing, and won't experience any unpleasant surprises in the middle of your work.

My hearty thanks go out to Peter Fronteddu and Stefan Steigerwald for their great devotion and excellent work. As author-photographer and knifemaker, they make an outstanding team!

As you use this book I hope your work is fun and successful!

Hans Joachim Wieland
Chief Editor, *MESSER MAGAZIN* (*Knife Magazine*)

Building a fully integral knife is really somewhat decadent. One cuts down a large (and depending on the material, very expensive) chunk of steel then works hard to fit the handle materials and attain general symmetry. And then the knife does not cut better than a flat-tang or stick-tang knife. In terms of balance and total weight, it cuts worse as a rule.

Yet it is fun to be irrational. It is the exclusivity and the knowledge of the higher expenditure of creative work that provides the charm.

For this book I made a knife almost completely by pure handcrafting, avoiding the machines I would otherwise be so glad to use. This was an experience that I am in no hurry to repeat. But it is also proof that the job can be done with simple tools. I have a lot of respect for anyone who sets out on this rough road.

I hope that through our instructions—which, as in our other books, are not absolutely required, but should serve as a guide to one's own manner of work—we have awakened the desire for a personal project.

The excellent photos and the step-by-step text for the three knife projects have, once again, been handled masterfully by Peter.

Stefan Steigerwald

As in the guides for backlock knives and making pocket-knives, I have documented each step of Stefan Steigerwald's process "live" in the workshop with my camera. Unlike the previous projects, in which we portrayed different variations in the operations but have essentially described a single knife, we have departed from that structure in this book.

The work methods for the knives shown here (filed, milled, wire-eroded) are so different that we have decided to show the work process for each of the three knives as completely as possible. Thus, after the basic considerations and creating the design, each knife is shown separately from the initial steps of the work to the finishing strokes. In Project I (hand-filed knife) we describe the work very thoroughly. For the other two knives, we concentrate on the special features of those production methods and deal in part with the steps that are also made for the filed knife. Thus it makes sense to read the directions for the filed knife (Chapter 3) before one goes on to the later chapters.

A layman like myself often does not realize what is behind handcrafting work. Now that I have been able to follow the complete creative process of demanding knifemaking work for the third time, I can appreciate the handiwork, the improvisational talent, and the creativity of a knifemaker much better. I hope that I have also been able to transmit that appreciation to the readers of this book.

Peter Fronteddu

PRELIMINARY CONSIDERATIONS

1.1 Several Paths—One Goal

Let us begin by clarifying the concept: An integral knife is a rigid knife in which the blade, choil, bolster (or guard), and pommel are made of a single piece of steel. So-called semi-integral knives (which have no pommel at the end of the handle) are differentiated from fully integral knives (which—as you thought—have a pommel). Integral knives are considered the most valuable of all rigid knives. In any case, they are the hardest to build.

There are many different methods for making an integral knife. To describe several different variations—starting from the same basic design—we shall build three integral knives. As in our earlier workshop books, we will start with a design and make a pattern for our integral knife.

Since not every knifemaker has an extensive machine shop at his/her disposal—and in any case, many adhere to working exclusively by hand—we shall show how an integral knife can be built using a minimum of machines. That is the first variation.

For a second knife, we shall utilize Stefan Steigerwald's customarily used "machine shop." It includes a plane-grinding machine, various belt sanders, borers, turning benches, and a large milling machine, with which the main part of the work on this variation of our integral knife will be done.

A further (and very unique) possibility is to have the raw knife wire eroded as completely as possible by a suitable outside technician. We shall also describe this method.

Just one note regarding work safety: Everyone who works on making a knife should be thoroughly informed about the necessary measures that make safe work possible and adhere to these measures. These include eye safety and securely attaching the piece to be worked on. These measures are especially important when motorized machinery is being used.

1.2 The Individual Knives

Our integral knife should have a practical size. It should remain somewhat handy but be fitted with a sufficiently large blade. We choose a blade length of 4 1/3" (11 cm) and about the same for the handle. As raw material for the filed and wire-eroded knives, we use a 1/2" ×1 1/3" (14 × 35 mm) piece of powder metallurgic RWL-34 steel, which we first shorten to the suitable length (with a little extra). For our milled project, we use a piece of rust-free Fritz Schneider Damascus steel of a suitable size.

The shapes and details of the knives depend on the possible ways to make them. For our file project we choose a typical drop-point hunting knife design. The blade shape and the grinding are good for practice and good results can be had working with a file. For visual reasons, we choose a slightly recurved shape. With the longer edge, along with a slightly rounded point, an ideal form for butchering wild animals results. The tapering rear portion of the blade is excellently suited for cutting or fine work. If one often cuts on a smooth surface or prefers a very classic hunting knife design, a drop-point blade with a straight cutting edge would be an alternative. The edge grinding should run all the way, until almost the base of the blade, which will produce a good cutting-edge angle and can be filed smoothly and simply. In general, we avoid complex shapes, so as not to make the work too laborious.

In our milling project we want to build a knife with Stefan Steigerwald's typical scale design. The spine of the blade has a false edge, the transitions of the scales and handle are rounded and given swallowtail passages. Along with the worked-in scales, the required work will become noticeably greater, thus we will do a lot with the belt grinder and milling machine.

From the wire-eroded raw piece, a very clear, rather "technical" design will result, appropriate for this knife, which is made primarily using machine production.

One thing in common with each design is that the pockets for the handle scales are made with an inclination toward the underside of the handle. The reason for this is that the scales can be fitted more easily and attached better that way. The angle locks them into the knife. This design is also more error tolerant—if one grinds a little too much off the scales, they slide a little deeper into the knife but do not fall through the pockets.

In a "scale knife," the pockets and scales are also made with a radius and a swallowtail passage, so that the correctly fitted scales can be turned into the pockets to make a firm, smoothly formed connection. The wire-eroded knife also has pockets with swallowtails.

Another design covered is the lanyard eye. Its contour depends on the end of the handle and runs parallel to the outer contour of the knife.

1.3 Choosing Materials

In an integral knife, the blade and handle form a unit. Thus to some extent different requirements apply to the choice of materials than to, for example, a jackknife.

• Since the blade and handle consist of the same material, its rust resistance takes on a special significance. The steel and the finish should be able to withstand hand perspiration longer, and their care and protection should be problem-free. This applies above all to the family of steels with a high chromium content (over 15%).

• At the same time, the steel should naturally hold its edge well.

• The steel should be easy to remove material from (with mill or file).

• The steel should allow a good finish.

• The hardener should have experience with the steel; faulty hardening should be avoided.

• The requirements for work on an integral knife are quite high. Thus it is not practical to save a little money on materials.

All in all, RWL-34 comes very close to these requirements, thus we have chosen this powder metallurgically made steel from Sweden. RWL-34 is sufficiently rust resistant, retains sharpness, and is very good to work with. Other highly alloyed steels, such as the CMP-S30V and S60V, are recommended for experienced metalworkers because they are more difficult to work with.

For the stainless variation of our integral knife, the scale knife, we will use a raw blank of rust-resistant Fritz Schneider Damascus steel. As one of the very few exceptions among the hand-forged Damascus steels, this one belongs to the group of rust-resistant steels. With a forged raw piece, one should first make sure that the size is sufficient for the planned knife. Often the pre-forged blade is not exactly straight and the surfaces are still rough and wavy from forging. All of that must be evened out, which reduces the external dimensions accordingly.

One should also make sure that the blank is still tempered to low tension after forging. In welded steels, more tension can build up from their many-layered construction than in one-piece steel. Thus one should also do everything while working it to counteract later hardness loss.

DRAWING A PATTERN

2.1 Project I: Filed Integral Knife

We'll draw—as our first reference point—the dimensions of our raw blank on paper. We determine the planned center (end of the hilt, beginning of the blade). The length of the edge (4 1/3" [110 mm]) and the hilt (likewise 4 1/3" [110 mm]) are determined and drawn in.

We determine the length of the edge—in our case about in the middle of the raw material.

We draw the outlines of the steel blank on paper in order to determine the maximum size of our design.

For the contour of the blade we use a helpful French curve. First we determine the upper edge of the blade, go on to draw the transition to the hilt on the upper edge of our limitations, and with the help of the stencil we design the upper edge of the hilt. The contour of the blade is drawn in freehand, here for our recurved blade.

The upper edges of the blade and hilt are laid out with the help of a French curve.

The blade contour is drawn in freehand.

Draw in the finger guard with the French curve.

We sketch the underside of the hilt.

Next we draw in the bolster with the finger guard. Here, too, we use a French curve to help make clean curves. The depth of the finger notch is equal to that of the rear end of the edge, so as to form an even line.

The lower contour of the hilt and the butt are drawn. Here, too, the upper edge of the finger notch is even with the roundings of the bolster and edge. In the rear area the hilt should not be made too pointed, otherwise there is a danger of the hilt material breaking off there. In addition, the knife would be unbalanced in the hand.

Draw the pockets into which the scales will later be set. The front edge runs parallel to the bolster. At the end of the hilt we decide on a 20-degree angle. The angle one chooses is a matter of taste and also depends on the basic design. In general, a pocket with an angle on at least one side is advantageous, because the scale material is easier to fit in. In a version with angles approaching each other, the scale material almost stays in by itself.

Finally, draw the lanyard eye and butt. We plan as big an eye as possible, since the weight of the butt is thus reduced and our knife lies in the hand with a better balance.

Determine the front and rear angles of the pocket for the scales.

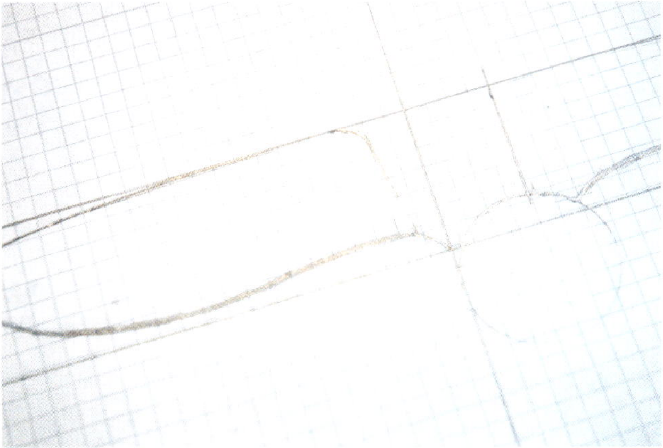

Draw the lanyard eye and butt.

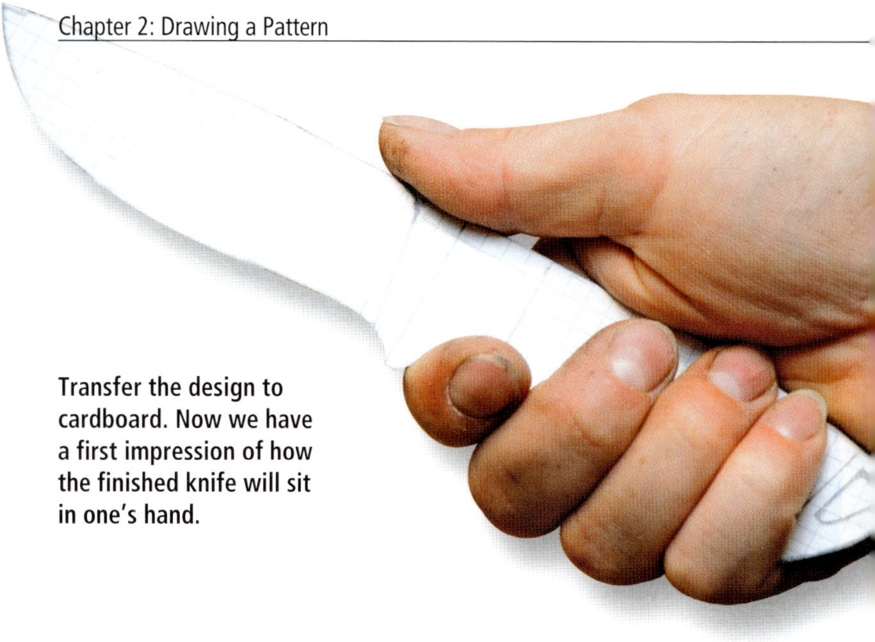

Transfer the design to cardboard. Now we have a first impression of how the finished knife will sit in one's hand.

Cut out the pattern and glue it onto stiff cardboard. Now we can test the hand position and see the proportions more clearly. If need be, we can adapt the pattern.

2.2 Project II: Milled Integral Knife

As with the filed project, we first make a pattern. Since we can work on this project on a milling machine with a round table, we choose a round milling with an added slant of 15 degrees for the pockets in the hilt. For this we use a specially ground swallowtail milling tool. Such tools are also available in the trade with larger angles, such as 25, 30, and 45 degrees. With sharp angles it will, of course, be harder in later steps to work out the transitions from the pocket to the scales symmetrically—especially toward the butt of the hilt and the underside of the hilt.

2.3 Project III: Wire-Eroded Integral Knife

For the wire-eroding project, a sketch with measurements is prepared. In our case two drawings are needed, first a view of the knife to provide the blade thickness, size, and shape of the scales and pockets. Since a lateral tilt is to be worked into the pockets, a side view will also be needed.

The drawing will be converted into CAD data by the contracted firm and the raw blank will be eroded according to our data. Since some of the arranging and transitional work is done away with by the eroding, we choose a more elaborate outside contour for this project. Thus, besides the angle, the blade also tapers in the direction of the point. Then the blade grinding will work out harmoniously toward the front later.

The swallowtail form of the pockets with 15 degrees and the transition radius are also made in this work step. The front and back of the bolster will be tapered to the ends of the hilt.

Thus the raw blank will show a contour after eroding in which no surfaces run parallel. For further work, we keep the separated parts of the blank—they will serve us later as a cutting guide.

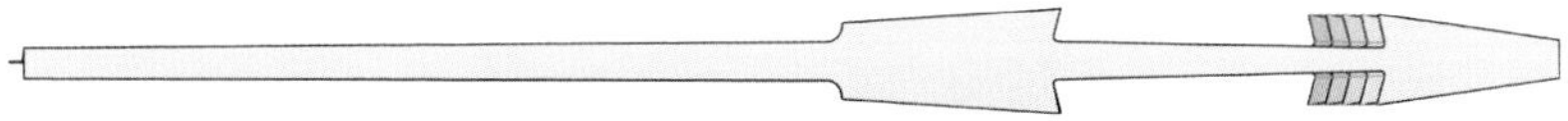

As a preliminary for the wire eroding, a hand drawing was prepared. This was turned into a 3D model and the coordinates were entered in the eroding machine.

The models show our integral knife from the top and at a high angle from the side. One can see the swallowtail shapes, which taper toward the pockets that narrow downward, and to the butt which tapers to the rear.

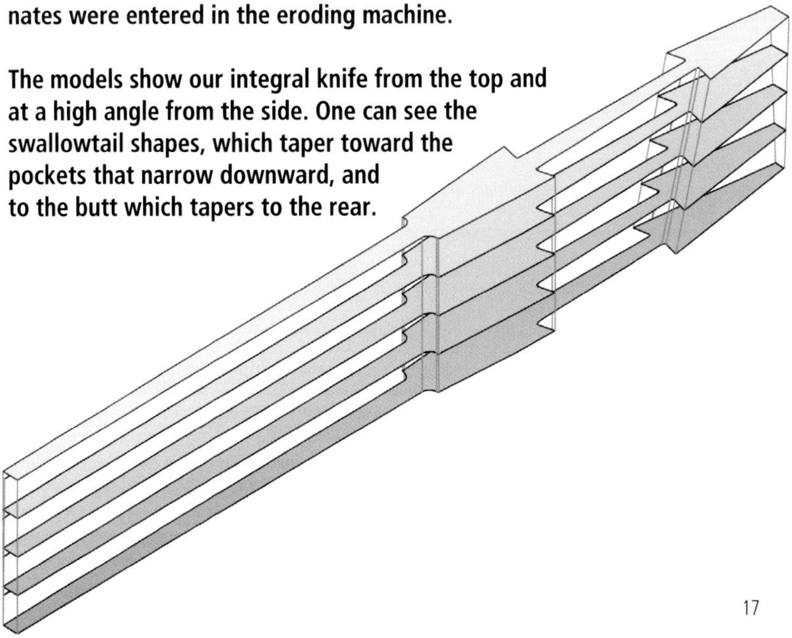

THE BASIC DATA FOR WIRE ERODING

When one has a knife blank prepared elsewhere, the saved time is a great advantage. With wire eroding, forms with angles and slopes can also be worked out very cleanly and symmetrically in a single process. Attaining the same precision by hand takes a long time and demands very precise work because of the many influential factors (cutting tolerances, rounding, and the transfer of the contours). Despite the not-so-modest cost of wire eroding, the outside work is worth the expense, especially for more elaborate knives.

There is a possible disadvantage, sometimes one side of a knife can be worked out completely by wire erosion which can allow tensions to build up in the material. Under certain conditions, these tensions influence the other side of the knife's ability to hold its shape. In addition, such tensions can later lead to distortion in the material during hardening.

This applies to all material-removing processes, thus also to CNC milling, and exactly the same if one manually completes one side of the knife at a time—either by milling machine or band cutter.

Therefore taking off material as equally as possible on both sides is recommended. This means, for example, one must alternate frequently in milling.

PROJECT I: FILED INTEGRAL KNIFE

3.1 Working on the Blade Surface and Pockets

Before we start, we place the pattern on our blank and, to be safe, check again to make sure our drawing fits on the blank. To prepare the blank, we first sand it so we can see the drawing lines better.

Measure the thickness of the blank and draw the centerline (make the line, turn the blank 180 degrees, and make the line again). Our blade should have a thickness of 0.177" (4.5 mm). Starting from the centerline, we mark 0.08" (2.25 mm) to the right and left of it. We also mark the end of the blade and the beginning of the bolster element.

First we sand the blank, so we can see the marking lines more easily.

The thickness of the blank is measured and the centerline is applied accordingly. We indicate the thickness of the blade by going outward from the centerline.

Since we want to work out the blank by hand, we limit ourselves at first to marking the end of the blade. Naturally, one could transfer the entire contour to the blank at once. Usually, though, the marking gets rubbed off or scratches when the blank is held and worked.

In addition, smaller changes can affect results in later steps, making the blade thicker or thinner than planned. We can still deal with that later when we lay out the haft.

Lay out the end of the blade. With the help of the pattern, we check the correct position again.

WHAT TO KNOW ABOUT FILES

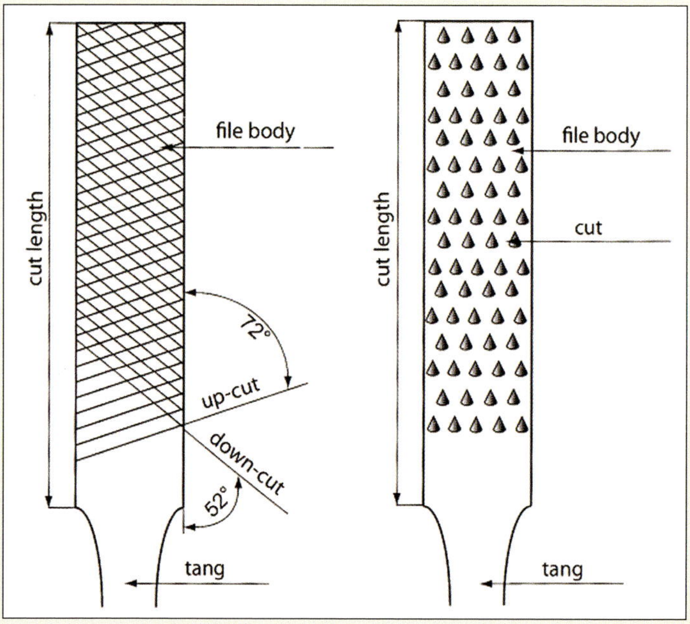

Files differ in their size, blade type, surface, and the form of teeth. Rasps, unlike files, have individual teeth. If the teeth are forged or cut (negative angle), they have a smoothing effect. Milled teeth (positive angle) have a cutting effect. Besides the profile of the teeth, files differ in the number and location of the teeth on the file surface.

The term "blade" indicates the whole area of the file teeth, which were made on the surface by forging, cutting, or milling. Basically, the harder the material being worked, a finer blade should be used.

For softer material, including softer metals, one can also use single-bladed files, in which a correspondingly greater distance between the teeth assures that the material does not get stuck and the file does not jam. For harder materials, two-bladed files are used. In these the so-called undercut has an inclination of about 50 degrees, and the overcut that crosses it has an angle of about 70 degrees. Thus the overcut forms the actual cutting surface; the intersecting undercut (usually set deeper and narrower than the overcut) is supposed to break the filings. Because of their angle to each other, the individual teeth are offset behind each other. This prevents scratches from being made in the material.

The cut number shows the number of teeth per centimeter, for rasps the number of teeth per square centimeter. The cut number serves to differentiate files. Ordinary files have numbers 00 or 0 (plane files for wood and soft materials), Cut 1 (coarser half-simple files), and Cut 2, 3, and 4 (simple files). Very fine precision files have cut numbers up to 10.

Files of the same cut number have different tooth numbers depending on their length. The number of teeth per centimeter is approximately:

Swiss-pattern Cut No.	American-pattern Equivalent	Tooth Number (Teeth per centimeter)
0	—	4.5 – 10
1	Bastard	5.3 – 16
2	Second Cut	10 - 25
3	Smooth Cut	14 - 35
4	—	25 - 50
5	—	40 - 71

Files are made with various cross-section shapes: Rectangular, triangular, round, diamond, and others. For flat surfaces one generally uses flat or half-round files; for the finger grooves on a knife, half-round files. For work on a ricasso one does best to use a file that has no teeth on one narrow side. Thus one can work on a blade without damaging the edge at the transition to the ricasso.

After being used, files should be cleaned regularly with a file brush to prevent material from getting stuck between the teeth. Otherwise a file will seem dull when next used.

3.1.1 The Blade Surface and Transition Radius

The first step is to take off as much material as possible. One possibility would be to bore holes along the outlines first and then to cut through them with a jigsaw, thus separating the excess material. The problem with this method for integral knives is that many holes with a diameter of some 0.118" (3 mm) must be bored precisely vertically over the entire width of the blank, thus 1.377" (35 mm). If one bores at an angle, one bores into what is later to be the blade, and the blank is spoiled.

Separate the excess material with a hacksaw just slightly off the outline. To be able to saw deeply, we turn the saw blade 90 degrees.

A hacksaw works best for this process. Parallel to the outline we saw off the excess material. Here we make sure that the saw blade does not stray and there is always enough distance from the outline (about 0.059" [1.5 mm] per side). At the outline of the blade end, too, we do not saw all the way to the marking, but leave enough space to be able to file the transition radius neatly later.

To be able to make a plane, we overcut the guard a little and span the blank so that the cut exactly matches the upper side of the guards. For exact arrangement, we knock the blank into position with a small hammer. This procedure—which is probably not in any textbook—spares us having to lay out auxiliary surfaces and file a plane surface freehand with the help of a hairline straightedge.

Separate the material with a transverse cut. We do not saw directly on the outline, but leave enough space to be able to work out the radius to the hilt neatly.

Sawing one side of the blank is finished.

Sand the guards a little to make sure that the two are parallel to each other. With a small hammer, set the blank up in the vise. The vise should be parallel to the upper edge of the guards.

You may have to file for a long time. File crosswise to be able to recognize the plane of the surface better.

Now it is time to file. By filing at an angle, we can ensure that the surface remains plane. We must work carefully with a flat file, especially at the radius (transition from blade to bolster). Twists are quickly filed into the radius. We file out the radius itself with a round file; the diameter is about 0.393" (10 mm). That automatically forms our transitional radius. The bolsters serve as lower contacts for working with the round file. Thus we make sure that we do not file too deeply at that point. After some two to three hours of filing work, the surface is finished and even.

With the round file we work on the transition from the blade to the hilt.

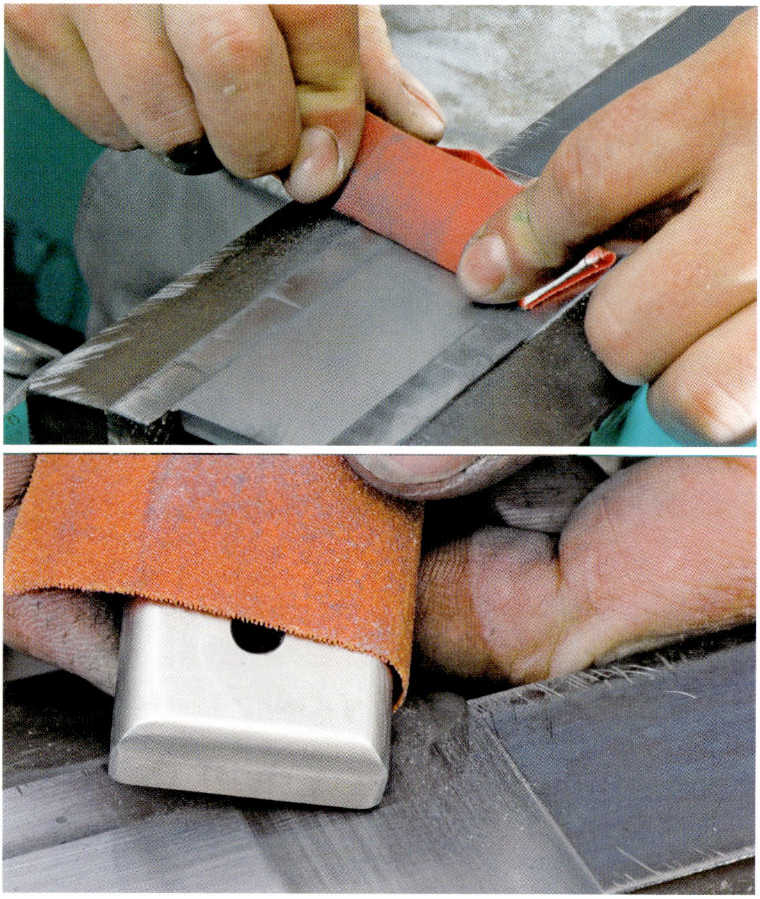

The surface of the filed blade is smoothed with a rounded sanding block and emery cloth (180).

Now we sand the surface clean with 120 or 180 emery cloth and a sanding block. For the transition we use an appropriately curved sanding block. Only the surface that remains after the sanding is really important in this work. For the fine work, one can concentrate on this area. The upper edge of the blade should also be made as clean as possible, since we orient ourselves to it later when we make the blade. When one side is finished, the opposite side can be made using the same steps.

Filed and finished—the blank and the tools.

3.1.2 Working Out the Pockets

After we have cut out the hilt contour, we file out the pockets. To work symmetrically, we work on one side for a little, put the blank in the vise along the cut lines, and carry the lines over to the other side. With the vernier height gauge we first lengthen the line of the blade to the end of the hilt.

Since we want to taper the tang to the butt, called a tapered tang, we do not cut this height line all the way to the back, but lower it about 0.039" (1.0 mm) in the rear area. When we sand and file the blank along this line, the desired taper results automatically.

Since our knife is to have a tilt of 20 degrees at the hilt end, we now make two auxiliary surfaces, so that the blank can be smoothed to the correct angle by filing upward.

By using the pattern, we draw in the sides of the pocket—the rear side at a 20-degree angle.

The blank is set in the vise so that work can be done on the blade surface and adjusted correctly with a small hammer. Here, too, our vise jaws serve as contacts or backstops. Now we file out the pockets for the hilt scales. At the front and rear sides we leave about a millimeter of material there. The ends will be finished in the next work step.

We put the blank in the vise so we can file parallel all around. With the help of a guide, we set the blank right at a 90-degree angle to the vise jaws.

The marked angles of the pockets.

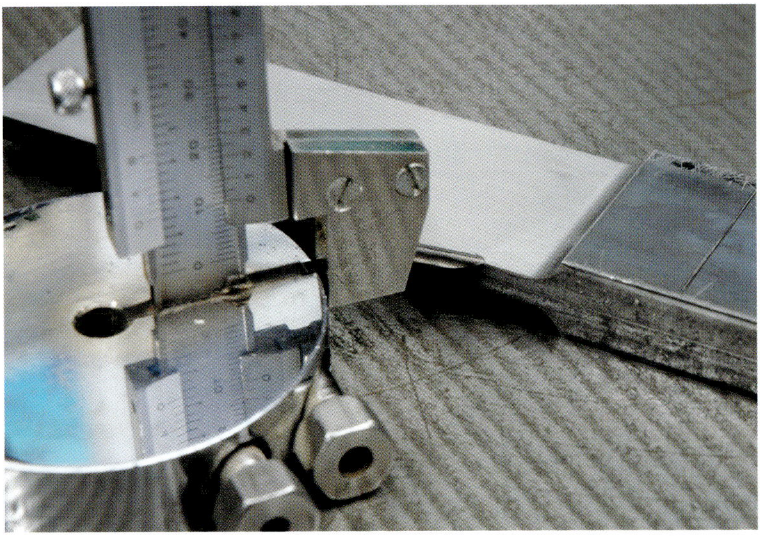

Cut out the pocket bottom. In the front area it should be on a level with the blade. We lower the back area about 0.039" (1.0 mm) and cut accordingly. This later affords a tapered angle.

To file the rear angles of the pockets at equal heights on both sides, we again use our vise jaws as contact points. For this, though, we must apply auxiliary surfaces at 90-degree angles to the slope (these surfaces are marked).

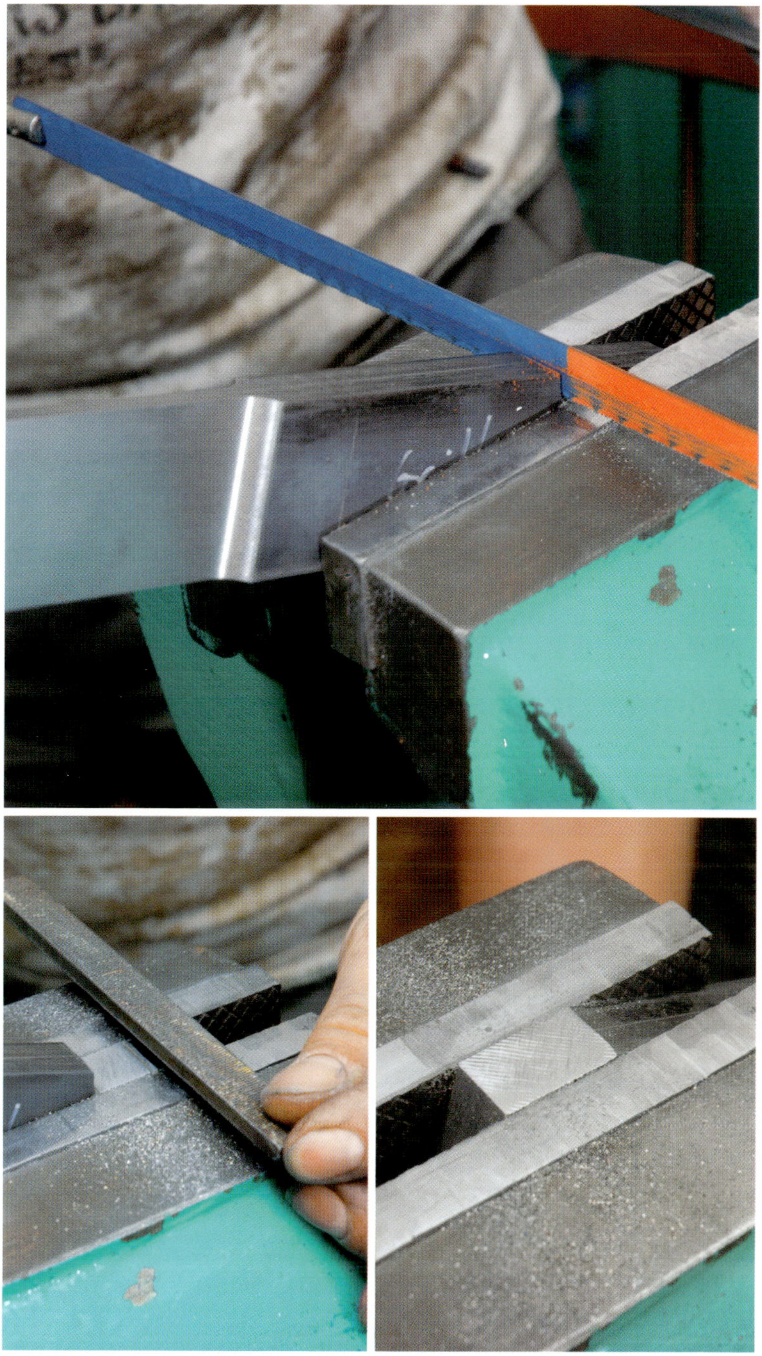

Saw and file the auxiliary surfaces.

To do this, we set up the blank at a high angle and file out the front and rear angles neatly. Now it is clear why we made our auxiliary surfaces: They serve as contacts for the rear angle. In this manner the blank is set exactly at a 20-degree angle. The filing is done again with the vise jaws as contacts. Mounting is done along the marked contour. We make sure that the blank is mounted exactly vertically. With a small hammer we correct it again if necessary. During filing, we make sure to keep the angle precisely.

The blank is set in the vise and arranged along the marked line.

File the pockets to the level of the vise jaws.

At the front and rear slopes we leave a little material. We will work this area out at a high angle in the next step.

The blank is mounted at the auxiliary surfaces. A guide is used to arrange the piece at the correct angle.

We file with the uncut side of the file toward the angle, so as not to damage the surface.

Finish the corners carefully with a finer file.

3.1.3 Making Protective Inlays

So far the blade surface and the tang have been worked out. In the next step we work out the outer contour. In order to keep sharp-edged transitions in the subsequent work and not round off the edges, we fill the pockets with protective inlays made of aluminum. This is also good practice for making the hilt material later.

The angle of the pocket is marked on the aluminum inlays.

Saw along the marked line. While sawing, we keep some distance from our marked line.

The dimensions and the angle of the butt are marked and the contour is cut out with saw and file. We make the two cuts match as much as possible, step by step, and make the screw holes for the scales. For safety's sake, we check the contour again before drilling and screwing the scales—the bored holes will later be covered by the hilt material.

We put the blank in the vise and again use the jaws as contacts and file the previously sawed edge down to a plane surface.

Interim result for the protective inlays.

To test them, we fit the inlays onto the blank.

A hole is bored through the protective inlays and the blank. Thread a hole and countersink it in the inlays. After assembly we will shorten the projecting bolts and file the surface smooth.

Draw the outer contour on the blank and the inlays. Mark the holes for bolting the inlays.

The bolt holes are drilled to fit the bolts. In our case a 0.157" (4.0 mm) hole is drilled through the inlay and the tang. On the other inlay we bore a 0.129" (3.3 mm) hole for the M4 threading.

Countersink for the bolt head with a countersink bit. Through the holes we drill the threadings for the inlay on the opposite side.

Bolt the inlays to each other.

Shorten the projecting bolts and file the inlays smooth.

3.2 Working Out the Outer Contour

After everything is completely mounted, we transfer the contour of the pattern onto our blank. The blank is then set in the vise with the protective inlays. We coarsely remove the excess material with a hacksaw. Then we work out the contour of the upper side of the haft with the file.

The knife's contour is drawn on the blank.

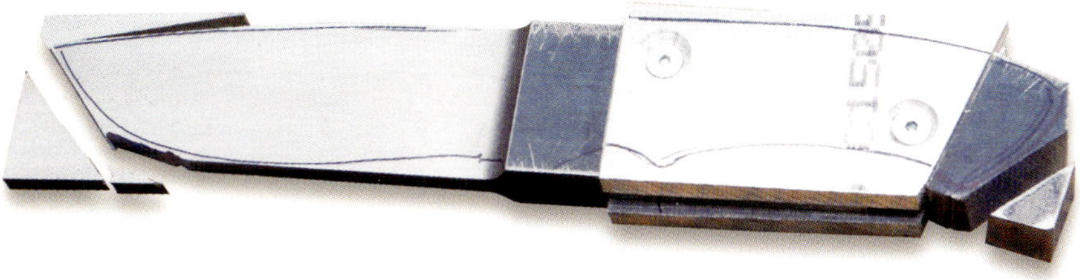

With a hacksaw we cut coarsely along the marked contour.

Work the upper side out coarsely with a file.

The closer we come to the contour line, the finer the work becomes.

Bore holes outside the line on the underside of the haft.

Since a lot of material is to be removed from the underside of the blank, we bore holes just outside the contour line. That saves time. With a hacksaw we cut through the holes. Continue the work with a file. We'll work out the finger grooves with a round file.

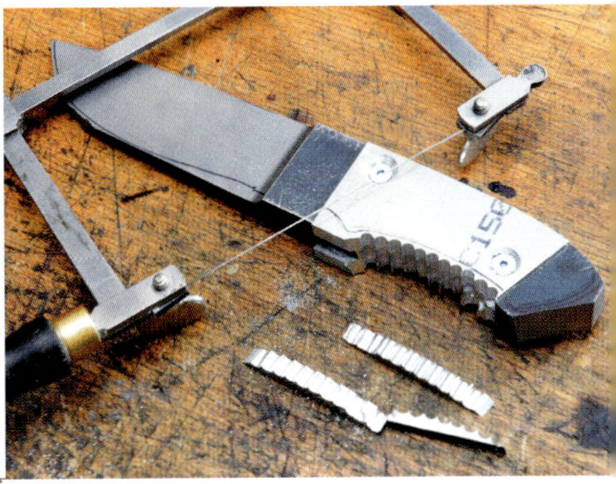

Cut through the metal with a hacksaw.

Use a half-round file for the underside of the haft.

Finish the knife contour all around with a file. For the forward finger groove, use a half-round file that fits the radius.

3.3 Working Out the Blade

We mark the middle of the blade's underside with a centerline. Thus we can see at once if we have struck the middle. Later we work on both sides, making the blade exactly symmetrical. To be able to see the marking more clearly, it helps to cut the blade angle even with the marking sooner. Alternatively, one can use a pen or paint to mark it.

To make the ricasso straight and symmetrical on both sides, we put the blank in the vise at the desired angle and mark the edge of the ricasso on both sides. Now both sides of the blade are filed. The upper edge of the blade and the marked cut line serve as orientation points.

The centerline is marked on the underside of the blade.

To draw the ricasso symmetrically on both sides, we set the blank in the vise at the desired angle and mark both sides.

Start working out the edge of the blade with the file. The ricasso, the centerline of the blade, and the upper edge of the blade serve as orientation points. Be careful to leave a neat upper edge.

We carefully work our way to the ricasso with a file, keeping the radius at the outer edge. Use a round file up closer to the desired edge.

We work carefully on the ricasso and leave some material there. Work out the transition from the blade surface to the ricasso with a round file. Continue the work with emery paper (to grade 240). For the fine smoothing on the ricasso we use a sanding block that we have prepared with a radius matching that of the ricasso.

After filing, we sand the blade in steps from P180 to P400, using a hard sanding block.

3.4 Working Out the Lanyard Eye

Paint the end of the handle with marking paint. Now draw the diagonals on. The contours run parallel to the outer edge of the hilt. Then transfer the form of the lanyard eye from the pattern to the blank with a marking needle. In the next step we will bore several holes within the contour. To bore them exactly vertically, our blank must sit absolutely flat with a suitable flat surface under it. With a hacksaw we cut out the excess material. Then we work out the contours with the round file. To keep the edges neat and avoid filing at an angle, use the jaws of the vise as contacts and screw in the blank accordingly each time.

The butt of the hilt is painted with marking paint.

The shape of the lanyard eye is transferred from the pattern. The contours should run parallel to the hilt.

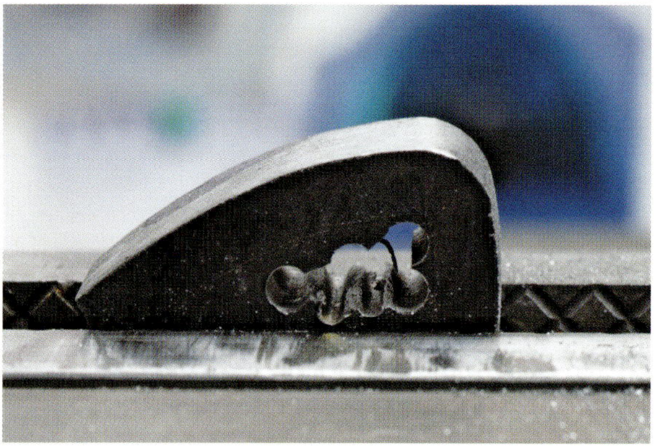

Drill holes and remove the material with a hack-saw.

File the inner contour of the eye.

3.5 Working Out the Hilt Contour

We begin by marking the centerline on the upper side of our blank. With the help of a pattern, the contours of the hilt are drawn to the right and left of the centerline. We use a French curve for marking the desired radius. This allows us to make sure there is symmetry along the centerline.

Put the blank in the vise. Work out the lateral surfaces of the hilt according to our markings.

Draw the centerline and the outer contours of the hilt.

File out the marked contour.

To file the front and rear inclines on the hilt, put the blank in the vise accordingly. The marked contour lines serve as contact aids.

Develop the hilt with a finer file.

In the next step we file a facet in the area of the bolsters. For this we put the blade back in the vise. On the sides of the hilt we mark the line at which our facet is to begin. On the top of the hilt we mark the desired depth. Work out the facet with the file. Make sure to work exactly along the marked edges.

Draw a facet, which serves as an aid in filing an evenly rounded shape later.

File the facet along the marked lines.

With a half-round file we then file the roundings on the finger grooves. At the butt of the hilt we break the edges and take off material corresponding to the marked contours. When working with the file, it helps to proceed piece by piece on both sides—frequently check the symmetry.

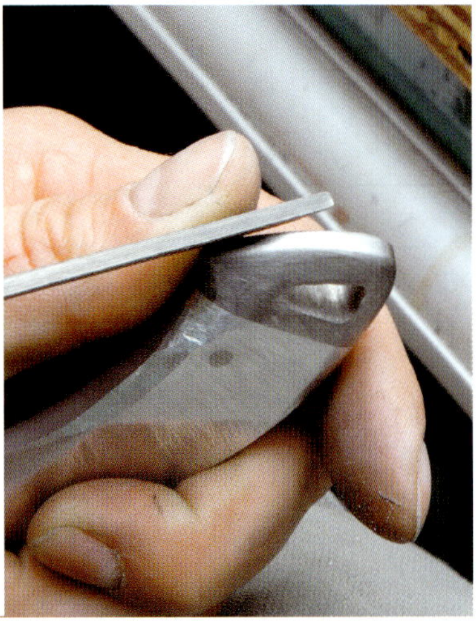

Working freehand, develop the surfaces into even roundings.

Round the edges at the butt end with files.

After we have worked out the contours, we round off the hilt neatly with a file. With emery paper and sanding blocks (matching the desired radii as needed), we finish smoothing the hilt. We work from P240 to 400, 600, and 800 and smooth alternating sides to check the raw depth. Only when the smoothing is completed with one grade do we go on to the next.

For the fine smoothing of the blade we use P400 grade paper, alternating the sides, and P600 for the final step. Don't forget to smooth the heel of the blade! Now the blank is finished and ready for hardening.

Use a hard sanding block to smooth the filed surfaces with P240 paper.

For rounding, we use strips of emery paper. The paper is less suited for a smaller radius.

Now that the butt end is rounded, we can also round the edges of the lanyard eye, first with the file, then with emery cloth.

3.6 After Hardening

Our blade is back from being hardened and is being tested for warping. There are various reasons for warping:

• Tensions present in the steel through rolling or shaping.

• Tensions released by shaping.

• Tensions caused by heat during shaping.

• Errors in hardening. The blade was unevenly heated or falsely positioned. Strong heat from nearby material can also cause warping.

A vacuum hardening oven in an industrial hardening facility.

A blade is tested for hardness after tempering.

Before continuing work on the knife, test the blank for warping.

Warped blades can be straightened by:

- A process of heating, straightening, and hardening
- Flame treatment
- Annealing packaging

Fortunately, our filed blank came back from hardening without any warping. Unfortunately, we forgot to bore out the holes for fastening the scales. We do that now with a 0.157" (4.0 mm) hard-metal drill. We drill carefully and cool sufficiently!

We draw the two scale holes in the middle. Bore the two holes with a 0.157" (4.0 mm) hard-metal drill. Then smooth them with a diamond file.

Mark the positions of the two holes on the wood for the scales.

In the next step we mark the shape of the handle scales on the wooden pieces. First, the angles of the pockets are marked on the material. Use the protective inlays to transfer the contours.

Use a hacksaw to cut the scale material along the marked angle. Put the scales in a vise at the desired angle to keep the angles correct during the ensuing work. This, again, creates a guide, limiting contact to just the right work surface.

Crudely cut the scales to the right shape with a hacksaw.

Put the scales in the vise along the indicated angle. Flatten the surface with a file.

Work out the front and rear edges of the scales step by step with file and emery paper. Regularly check that the scales maintain a firm fit in the blank. Here we see the advantage of not making pockets with 90-degree angles: The hilt material is held in place by the angles of the scales. Small errors can be corrected; if one has taken off too much material, the scale slides farther into the pocket but does not fall out toward the bottom.

We smooth the scales to fit, using up to P180/P240 paper. On a suitable flat base, we also smooth the underside. Be sure to regularly check the scale's fit in the pockets.

Smooth the filed surfaces.

After every work step, check how the scales fit in the pockets.

On a flat base smooth the undersides of the scales.

Checking the fit of the scales.

When the scales are smoothed suitably, glue one scale on with epoxy resin adhesive. Press the scale on firmly and make sure that it sits evenly at all points. Examine the fit with a magnifying glass. A clamp provides constant high pressure while the parts set.

Using the holes we already drilled in the knife for our hilt bolt we now drill 0.157" (4.0 mm) attachment holes through the scales. The scale on the other side is prepared the same way and glued on. Now we drill completely through both scales and countersink the holes to the diameter of the rivets—here 0.236" (6.0 mm).

The scale is glued on and a clamp is attached.

Drill 0.157" (4.0 mm) holes through the wood using the holes in the tang.

Glue the scale on the other side.

Now drill all the way through.

With a 0.236" (6.0 mm) countersink, deepen the holes for our bolts.

Check the length of the rivets and shorten if necessary. For screwing them, we saw a groove. Now the bolts are mounted and the scales thus attached. In the next step we will file the hilt into shape. We do not work all the way to the steel, but leave some material—some 0.003" to 0.007" (0.1 to 0.2 mm)—in place. The fine work will be in the next step.

Check the length of the hilt bolts and, if need be, shorten to fit.

With a hacksaw we cut a slit for the screwdriver.

We secure the bolts with securing paint and tighten them.

Shape the scales with a file. We do not work all the way to the steel, but leave some material there to retain clean transitions for the fine work.

Round off the profile more cleanly. Here too, we do not work to the steel.

3.7 Finishing

Bring the scales into shape with fine files and sandpaper. Work carefully on the transitions between the scales and pockets. The steel surfaces between the scales are hardened, of course, but one should still not go over this surface with a sandpaper that is too course. In the first steps, sand the scales up to P240, not all the way through each of the papers. If we did, we would risk letting the hilt material be sanded away faster than the steel, and the transitions between the scales and the knife would become messy. Only in fine sanding with P400 and P600 do we work down to the steel.

In sanding over the grip bolts, too, make sure not to take away too much of the surrounding material. Thus we use hard sanding blocks for this step. We smooth the grip carefully to 1200 grade and then evenly take off the guard and butt pieces in this step. Since the surfaces are mostly uneven, it makes sense to stretch the emery paper over a somewhat softer sanding block

We file the contour further. In the process, we make sure not to work down to the level of the steel.

for the last sanding step. To be sure, this is only for the metal surfaces. The transitions and grip scales would be sanded down too quickly, and the transitions would become messy.

Wrap the handle with a rag and put in the vise. Only satinize the blade with 800 grade sandpaper. In so doing, always use fresh sandpaper and always rub in only one direction, without taking it off. To make a good finish is not simple, and every knifemaker has his/her methods. Our knife is finished with 800 grade sandpaper, and finally worked with fine paper (used 800) and diamond paste.

One can also smooth cleanly with P400 and then go over it a couple times with P1200. This must, of course, be done very carefully; otherwise shining spots will occur. Or one thus sands up to P1200 and leaves it at that. The choice of sanding blocks can also be important. For the last strokes we use a thinly glued block (bicycle inner tube). Here too, one must be careful not to make the edges round.

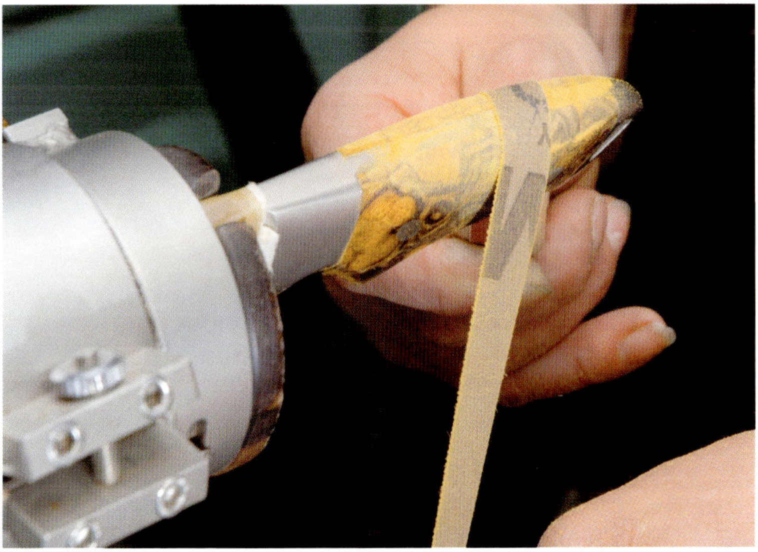

Round the handle with strips of emery cloth.

With P400 to P600 paper on a hard block, smooth the scales down to the steel. Then smooth finely up to P1200.

The blade is satinized in even strokes with 800 emery paper.

In the last work step, place the knife on a soft surface so that the emery paper can be applied thoroughly over the full surface. This makes a more even surface. Here too, we make sure to retain transitions and edges and not to smooth them round.

We smooth the radii of the ricasso and the butt by dipping the edge of the sanding block into the blade.

To apply a logo, we use an electrochemical etching process.

An engraving or etched logo looks good and works well on monosteel (in our case RWL-34). First we work with equal tension (12-18 volts and 2-4 amperes) and put the positive pole at the end of the knife. Thus we assure good contact, and avoid burned spots. The negative pole is placed on a graphite block with a felt cover. The felt is moistened with a special electrolyte. Attach etching foil to the desired position on the blade. Now press the negative end with the block on the foil, but not for too long to avoid too much heat. After pressing the block on a few times, a very deep impression results. To achieve more contrast in the logo, switch the electric power to alternating current and press it on again briefly.

The pattern is positioned and, under pressure, a stamp with electrolyte liquid is pressed on.

The logo right after the etching. One can see the blurred appearance.

Satinize the blade again with 800 paper and diamond paste to make the lines of the logo appear crisper.

Before sharpening, treat the handle. Wax products in particular are recommended for tropical ironwood, so as to avoid darkening as much as possible. The final step is to sharpen the blade with a diamond sharpener.

In the last step we sharpen the blade with a diamond file.

Our finished filing project—a classic hunting knife.

PROJECT II: MILLED INTEGRAL KNIFE

4.1 Milling the Blade Surface

As with the file project, we mark the centerline of the knife and work on the blade first. Those familiar with milling machines usually know how to complete this task. We have decided to work with a milling roller with a round hard-metal cutting plate. With it one can, in one step, also work out the transition radius from the blade to the hilt.

The blank is clamped onto the work table with clamps. A contact surface is fastened in back; it will help us later in preparing to mill the other side.

The underside is already finished. To avoid fluttering, suitable padding material is clamped on at the point of the blade.

The clamped-down blank in the second milling.

One side is now milled. Mark the extent of the transitional radius, set the indicator at zero, as well as the depth setting. Both will be needed later for milling the other side. The point of the blade must again be clamped down. Or one leaves a surface for smoothing and works out the point of the blade separately. While milling the other side, we clamp down the blank with sufficient padding under the surface that has already been milled.

4.2 Milling the Pockets

Our pocket is equipped with a radius that will later be given a swallowtail pattern. The handle material must thus only be fitted and glued. Without turning, it cannot fall out of the pocket any more. The scales of our knife will also be secured with a pin.

We mark the contour of the pockets on the sides of the blank and also mark the depths. For the planned radius with a swallowtail pattern, we make use of the middle point and drill or

Using our pattern, we lay out the middle of the pockets and punch.

smooth with an attaching aid. The hole must, naturally, be within the handle contour.

The tang of our knife should taper toward the rear (tapered tang). To prepare the pockets suitably, the blank is mounted at an angle. We raise the rear side of the blank a little with an underlay (~0.023" [0.6 mm] thick), secure it with a pin through our attaching aid, and clamp the blank in.

Drill and smooth a center hole so the piece can later be placed on the round milling table.

To be able to see the markings better, we coat the blank with marking paint.

Using the height marker, we take the measure of the blade and mark the thickness of the tang accordingly on the front part of the handle.

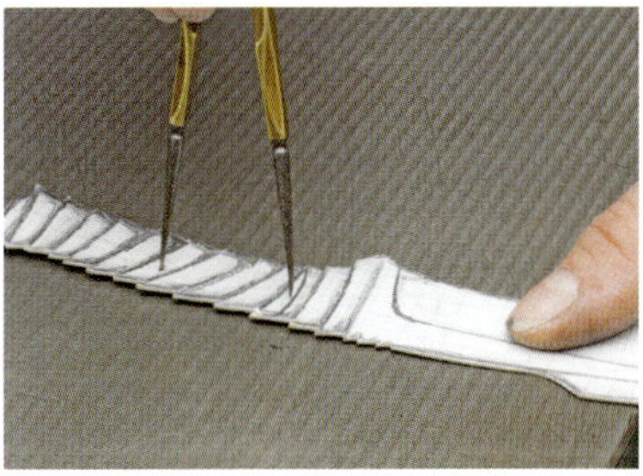

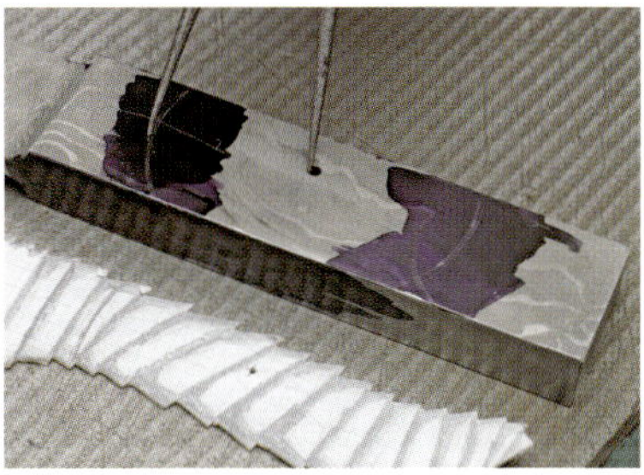

With the help of the pattern, we set the desired radius of the pockets and transfer it to the blank.

The rear part of the blank is fixed on the round table at the correct angle for the tapered butt with the help of an underlay.

We mill until almost the marked depth and also mill the radius.

The middles of the pockets are milled.

We finish the inner contour of the pocket with the swallowtail mill.

First we mill with a turning-plate mill to just short of our desired contour. We mark the coordinates for the opposite side. Then we finish milling the edges of the pocket with a 15-degree swallowtail mill. Here, too, we note the measurements.

One pocket is milled and finished.

Before we attach the blank, we remove edges and uneven spots.

When one side is finished, we smooth the surface plane. Now we attach the other side and mill the other pocket in the same way.

Work out the second pocket in the same way.

Finally, we check the symmetry of the pockets.

4.3 Making Protective Inlays

So as not to risk our neat edges in subsequent work, we make—also on the round table—aluminum inlays that fit into the pockets. Thus one gets an impression of how good the swallowtail form will hold the handle material.

Transfer the radius of the pockets onto cardboard and make a pattern for the protective inlays. Contours are transferred from the pattern onto an aluminum sheet and worked out on the milling machine. For protection, and for a better plane surface, we attach the scales to an underlay.

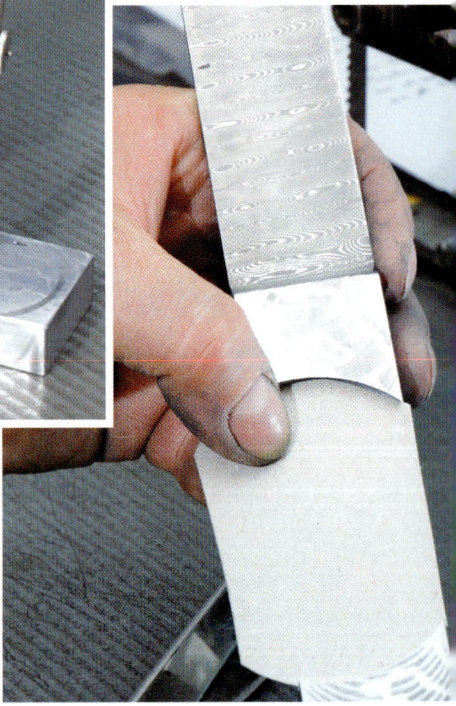

With a compass we crudely mark the radius of the pockets. Transfer this to a cardboard pattern and check the fit.

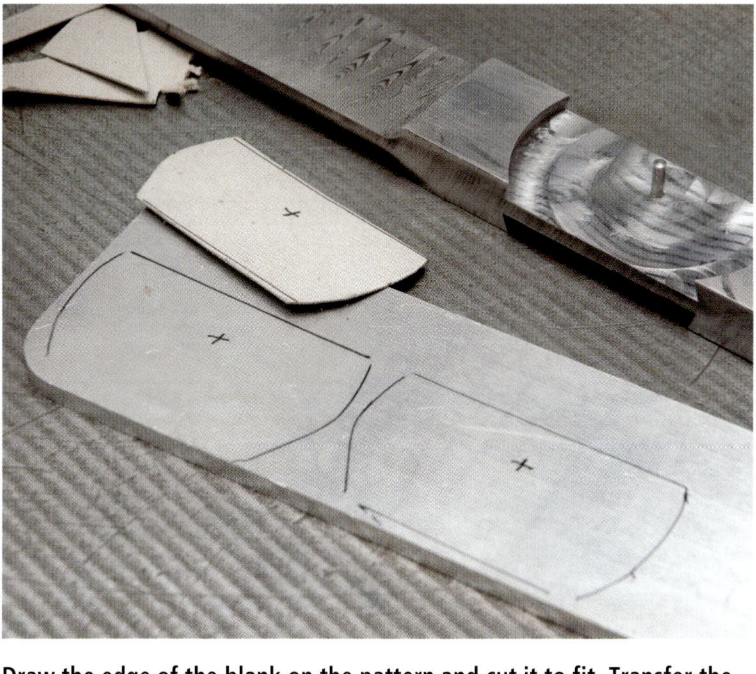

Draw the edge of the blank on the pattern and cut it to fit. Transfer the pattern to a suitable filling material (sheet aluminum, brass).

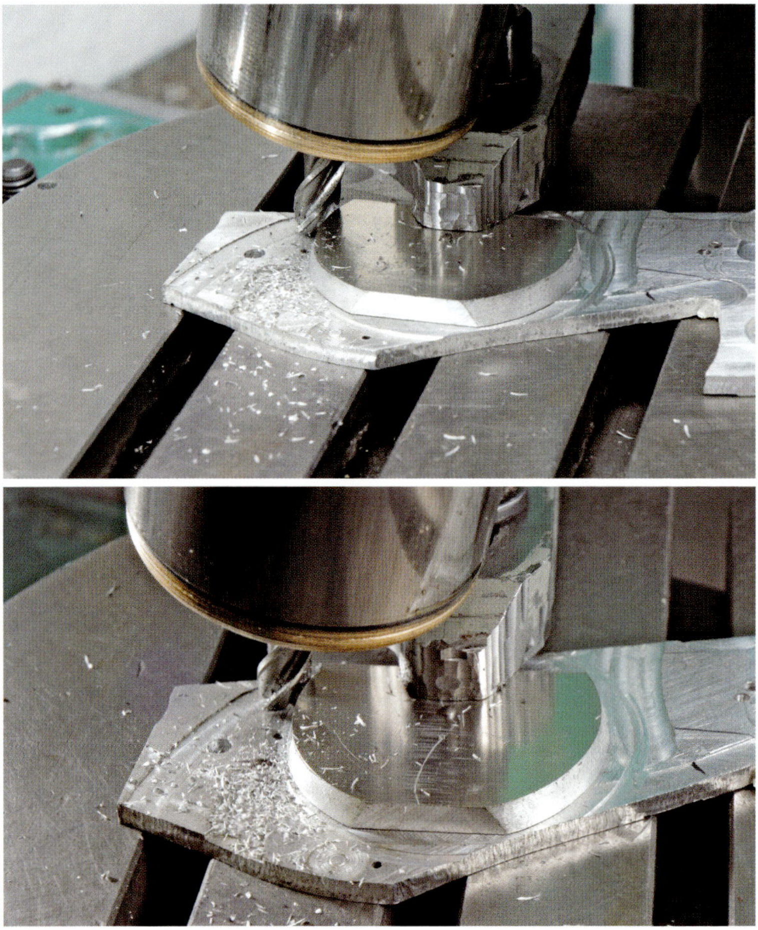

With its head set at an angle (15 degrees), we mill the radius of the protective inlay. The sheet aluminum was fastened on a protective underlay and fixed with a pin, as in the work on the blank.

Check the fit of the protective inlays. With an exact fit, the inlays will only loosen from the pockets by being twisted. Thus we do without bolts and secure the inlays with super glue, which we let flow into the gap between the inlays and the blank on both sides.

After mounting and securing, we paint the blank with marking paint and lay out the contour from our pattern.

Test the fit of the inlays.

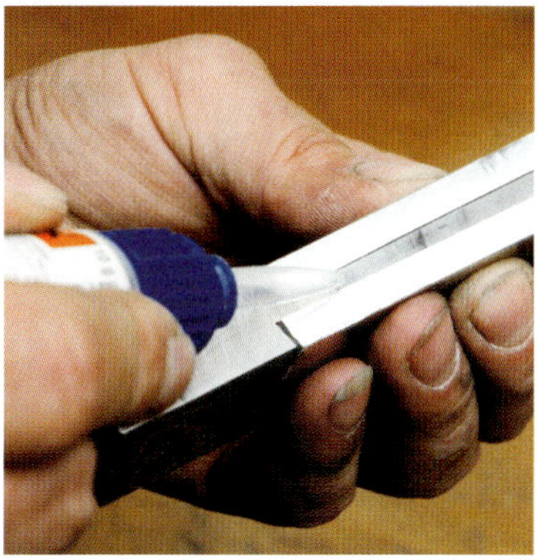

The protective inlays are held only by super glue.

Coat the blank with marking paint and transfer the contour from the pattern with a marking needle.

4.4 Working Out the Outer Contour

With the angle grinder, we remove excess material. The belt sander, with which we work out the contour, takes the job farther. We use a belt with 40 grain. On the upper side of the blank and in the blade area there is relatively little material to remove, so we only work with the belt sander. Mark the edges where Stefan Steigerwald's signature "scales" will later be worked out. We take care to stick carefully to the edges and not to make them round. Later we will work further on the scales with a file and a milling machine.

Work out the knife's contours crudely with an angle grinder. This saves time and belts for the belt sander.

The knife after preliminary cuts with the angle grinder. Additional work is done on the belt sander.

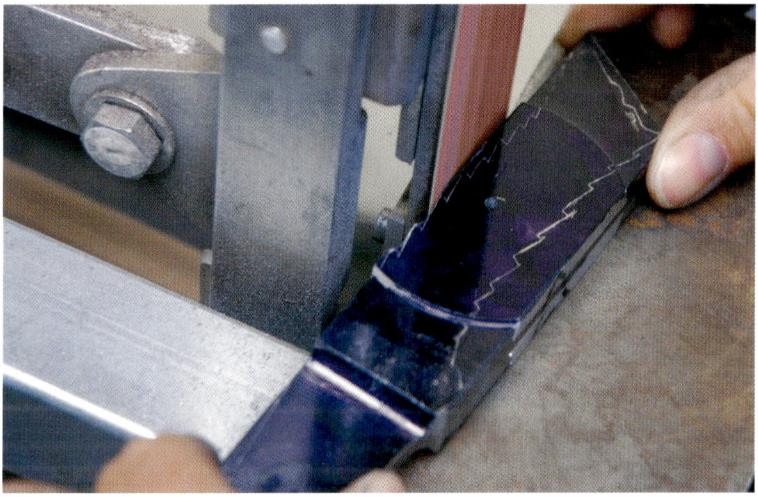

With a 60 band we grind along the contour.

Since a lot of material is to be removed from the underside, we bore a few holes to make the work easier. This method goes faster than removing the material with a belt sander and spares the belt and the machine. Now we use the belt sander to work out the lower contour and the butt of the handle.

To spare the belt sander, we drill holes on the underside to remove as much material as we can.

Work on the contour continues with the belt sander.

4.5 Working Out the Blade

We have already begun to work out the outer contour. The protective inlays are now mounted, and the knife is coated with marking paint. Now we mark the contours of our grinding with the marking needle, beginning at the end of the blade, by the ricasso. To work symmetrically, we fasten the blank in the vise and mark both sides.

Transfer the lines (height line, blade, ricasso) to the blank so we can work out the blade.

Mark the ricasso in the vise to make it symmetrical on both sides.

Transfer the height line for grinding the blade from the pattern to the blank.

Place the blank in the vice at the level of the marked height line and mark the line on both sides as far as the tip of the blade.

Then we mark the height of our blade. The cutting line should run straight and remain at the same height all the way to the point.

In the forward area we mark the bend in which the upper edge of the grinding is to end. This runs upward out of the blade parallel to the cut. The middle of the cut is marked.

With a compass we lay out the upper edge of the bevel. The line runs parallel to the edge of the blade.

The middle of the blade is marked mechanically. By marking on both sides, possible unevenness becomes visible.

We work out the bevel on the belt sander. We must be sure to work as exactly as possible along our marked edges without going over them. In the ricasso area we use only a flexible P150 grinding band, which we let overlap the contact wheel some 0.118" to 0.196" (3 to 5 mm). Thus the grinding band is mounted flexibly, and it results in an optically striking transitional radius when ground.

While working with the band grinder, we leave a little material in the area of the ricasso. Here, too, we want to maintain an exact radius and neat edges—later we will work this area with a sanding block and sandpaper.

On the contact wheel of the belt sander we gradually grind out the high cut against the blade edge. We work step by step and constantly check the results.

While grinding, the marked edges must be kept exactly. Continually check the symmetry of the two sides.

Secure the blade in the vise and smooth. Work lengthwise to the blade. For the transition at the ricasso we use a sanding block with an appropriate radius and let the sandpaper hang over it slightly.

At the point of the blade, let the taper run out upward to the spine of the blade. To retain a neat grinding edge, we must take off some material in the upper area of the blade. We coat the blade with marking paint and mark the desired blade on it. Remove the material with a file. We must be sure to work as exactly as we can along the edge. Then we smooth it with a sanding block—lengthwise to the blade, thus perpendicular to the traces of grinding.

For smoothing we use a sanding block that matches the radius of the contact wheel.

The blade is smoothed lengthwise with up to P240. To smooth the ricasso, we let the sandpaper hang over slightly.

The height line is marked again to the tip of the blade.

Above the height line we narrow the blade tip somewhat and smooth it.

In the extension to the spine of the blade, the lower edge of the false edge, which projects upward, is marked and worked out exactly to the edge with a file. To grind both sides symmetrically, we use the marked centerline of the blade for orientation. After that we smooth by hand with up to P240.

Mark the lower edge of the false edge.

Put the blank in the vise vertically. For subsequent work, the marked centerline helps with orientation.

We work out the false edge with a file, making sure the edges are neat.

After filing we smooth it with P240 grain.

4.6 Working on the Hilt Contour and Lanyard Eye

Since the exact contour of the lanyard eye is formed only after the scales are finished, we now focus on the hilt. We remove the drawing paint and unglue the blade in order to protect it while working with the belt sander. Our “scales” are transferred from the pattern to the handle of the blank. Work out the contour crudely with the belt sander.

The marked lines are a good indicator of the results we are aiming for.

We work out the contour with the belt sander freehand. The scales are smoothed all around, section by section.

Our fully ground blank already looks very interesting.

Use files for the fine work on the scales. We work as neatly as we can—especially on the edges and transitions. The protective inlays are removed later, but the upper and lower sides of the blank are already worked out in this work step. On the hilt we work step by step and constantly check the symmetry.

We round everything off evenly with the file.

As with the filed knife, we now draw the desired contour of the lanyard eye. We drill two holes inside the contour and cut out the material between them with a coping saw. Use a file to give the eye its desired form. Then file the inside of the lanyard eye with a fine file.

The lanyard eye is drawn on the butt of the handle.

So the drill does not slide on the rounded surface, we use a center drill bit for the initial bore then we drill all the way through with a normal bit.

Use a coping saw to cut out the metal between the drill holes.

Smooth the interior surface of the lanyard eye with a file.

Smooth the handle once more with P240.

After filing, we finish smoothing the handle. We work with a sanding block and paper of P240, 400, and 600 grades. We also finish smoothing the lanyard eye. For that we use strips of sandpaper, increasing the grade as when smoothing the handle.

We also work on the blade area with sandpaper up to P400 or 600. When we change the grade, we also change the direction of motion. This allows us to see that the smoothing has been done completely. The blank is then set in a vise and padded with a cloth to avoid damage.

We smooth the blade up to 600 grade.

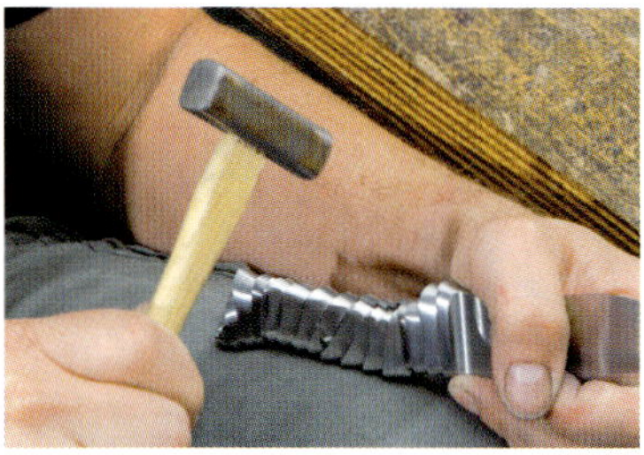

With a small hammer the protective inlays are carefully removed.

Our blank is ready for hardening.

After this step, the protective inlays are carefully removed. When installing the protective inlays earlier, we drove in a pin, around which the inlays can be turned out of the pockets. Carefully, we knock the inlays out without damaging the edges of the knife. The blank is now ready for hardening.

4.7 After Hardening

After hardening, the handle scales are finished. First we transfer the contours from the protective inlays to the hilt material. We make sure that there is still enough material present around the contour on the hilt material to leave room for fitting.

The position of the central drill hole is transferred from the protective inlays to the scales. Drill a hole 0.039" to 0.118" (1 to 3 mm) deep to hold a pin. With it we can work step by step on the round table and can always attach our bolsters in the right place after every work step.

We transfer the contour of the scales from the protective inlays to our hilt material. The central drill hole was also marked, so the scales can be attached on the round milling table.

Cut out the scales crudely with a hacksaw and then put them on the round milling table. Use the shaft miller on the scale blank similar to the work on the pockets. Now we mill the front and rear contours of the scales. We work step by step and carefully make sure we achieve as exact a fit as we can. After every step we test the fit of the scales in the hilt. The scales should sit as tightly as possible.

We drill holes for the centering aid.

We do the crude work with a hacksaw.

We mount the scales on the round milling table and mill the contours with a head set at an angle of 15 degrees.

After the first milling we measure the scale and compare the dimensions with the inlays.

The fitted scales are now rotated into the hilt. If their fit is very stiff, we can help it cautiously with a small hammer. As soon as the scales sit properly, we check the whole thing again for cracks or a poor fit. Then the scales are attached with super glue.

We work in small steps and check the fit regularly. When the scales sit firmly without give, they are rotated into the pockets.

If need be, we help them with light taps with a hammer.

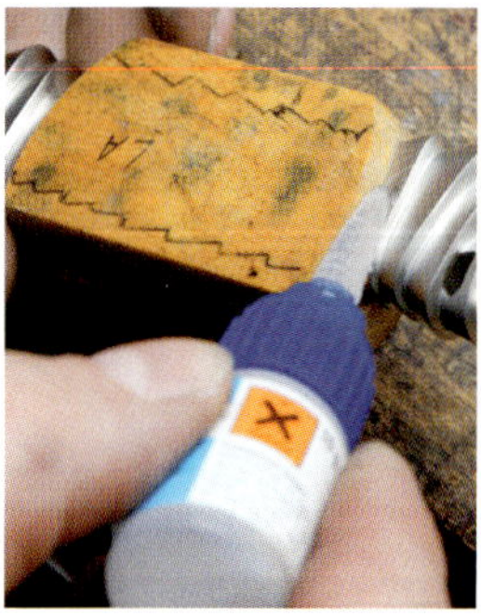

Attach the scales with super glue.

Work out the rough outer contour with the belt sander. Draw the pattern on the scales with a pencil, and file them out by hand. After filing, it is time to finish them.

Using the belt sander to work out the contour of the scales.

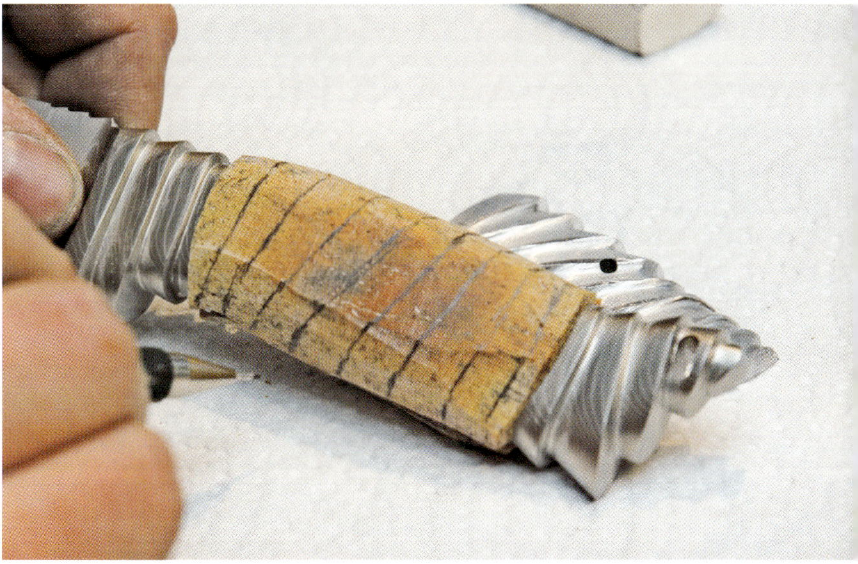

Draw the scale pattern on.

Form the scales' scales with a file.

4.8 Finishing

For working the blade, tighten the knife in a vise or clamp. Wrapped in a cloth and held only by rubber pads, the handle is surely safe from damage. We satinize the blade with P600/ P800 paper and always work in just one direction, toward the point.

We begin on the scales with P240, but leave enough material over the handle contour so as not to mar the transitions. Only in fine sanding with P400 and P600 do we work out neat transitions.

The scales of our knife and the surrounding metal are smoothed only in the direction of the scales. To make sure that we do not overlook any area while smoothing, we paint the surfaces to be smoothed with pore filler or fast-smoothing base after every change of paper grade. We smooth the handle material and then the entire knife clean up to P800.

Clamp down the blade and satinize to P800.

To make the structure of the Damascus steel stand out, the knife is etched. The scales are protected with suitable covering paint. The Fritz Schneider Damascus of our knife is etchable with iron trichloride. Normal nail polish is sufficient for protecting the scales. The transitions from the handle material to the knife must be very carefully covered, though we cut off the paint on the blade with a scalpel after it dries.

Various protective paints for other etching methods are found in the cosmetics industry (red covering paint) or art supply goods (asphalt paint = bitumen paint). To what extent the paints are resistant to the acids we use should be tested on test pieces first.

With a sanding block and 240 grade sandpaper continue smoothing the surfaces.

At P600 we smooth down to the steel.

Cover the surfaces that won't be etched with nail polish.

The overlapping paint is removed carefully and precisely with a scalpel.

For etching we use a sufficiently large glass and put it in a pail filled with warm water. This has two advantages: The warmth speeds the process, and the pail catches any dripping acid.

After a few minutes of effecting time, we pull the knife out of the bath and rinse it a little for neutralization. For surface cleaning we wipe the knife off with a cloth and check the depth of the etching with a fingernail. Repeat the process according to how the acid "eats" and how deep you want the etching to be.

After etching, rinse and clean the knife thoroughly. The protective paint is removed with a suitable solvent (turpentine, thinner, spirits). Has the protective paint done its job? If not, one can carefully smooth over the area and then polish it.

Work the etched surface again with the finest sandpaper (such as used old P2000). Thus the pattern still stands out with sharp edges.

After the knife is cleaned with acetone (caution, do not wipe the nail polish off again!), the knife is hung in the acid bath.

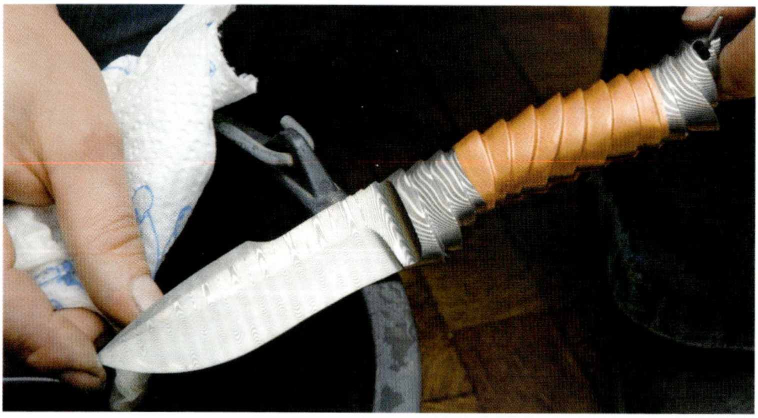

We regularly check the progress of the etching. When the steel has enough marking, we rinse it in clear water.

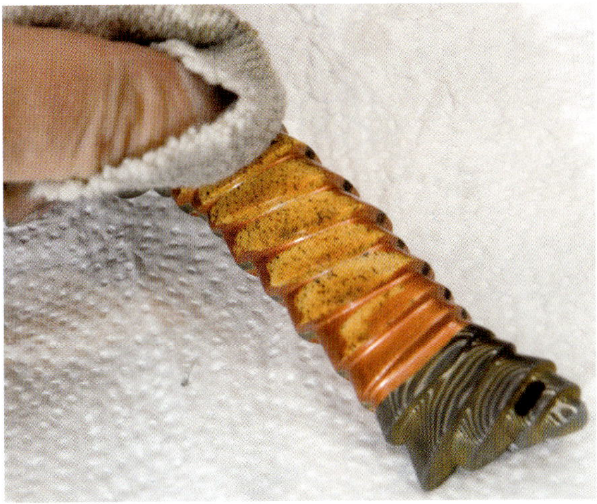

Remove the protective paint.

After etching, the knife is still somewhat matte. Smooth the surface with P2000 paper.

To enhance the optical effect, smooth the blade surface with P800 and diamond paste.

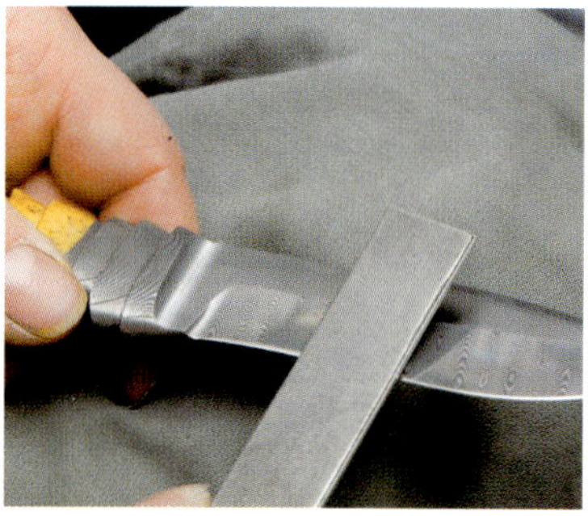

Finally, sharpen the blade with a diamond file.

Smooth the surface and carefully polish the knife again.

Sharpen the knife with a diamond file. Polish the handle again by hand or smooth it very fine and maintain with flax oil wax products, Danish Oil, or shellac polish. The shinier the finish is, the more sensitive it is.

In the last work step, we engrave a logo on with an engraving machine. To let the structure of the Damascus have its effect, we do not put the logo on the blade surface, but on the back of the knife.

An engraving machine adds Stefan Steigerwald's logo to the back of the blade.

The finished integral knife with Steigerwald's signature scale design.

PROJECT III: WIRE-ERODED INTEGRAL KNIFE

Most of the work steps we have already described are omitted since we will have the blade blank prepared in advance. In this case the blank was wire eroded. The blade area was tapered sufficiently. The pockets for the scales, including the swallowtail shapes, were cut. The handle contour—our handle is somewhat thicker in the middle and tapers to the front and back—has already been prepared.

Pockets, blade contour, tapered butt. After wire eroding, the blank comes to us almost finished.

5.1 Making the Protective Inlays

For this blank, too, we make suitable protective inlays on the milling machine, as described in Chapter 4.3 for the milled knife. The inlays are set at angles and held by the swallowtail cuts and super glue. The protective inlays protect the pockets during subsequent work.

As in the milled project, we make suitable protective inlays on the milling machine. The inlays are held in with super glue.

5.2 Working Out the Outer Contour

The outline of our knife is transferred to the blank. Cut off excess material crudely with an angle grinder. Work out the outer contour on the belt sander with a band of P40 grade paper. On the underside of the handle, on the groove, we leave some material. We will mill out this area in the next step.

Using a pattern, we draw the outlines of our knife on the blank.

Remove as much material as possible with an angle grinder.

Work out the contour further on the belt sander.

Before we mount it in the mill, check that the blank matches the pattern and, if necessary, make more markings. The blank is suitably wedged on the sides—we use the scrap pieces from the eroding process as wedges—and screwed into the machine's vise.

Work along the indicated contours with the radius miller. Thus the surfaces as well as the transitions to the butt end and crossguard are finished in one step. Afterward we grind the surfaces by hand, up to P240, on all sides of the blank.

Before we put the blank in the mill, we check the contours against our pattern again.

The blank is suitably wedged when attached to the mill. With the roller mill we mill the surfaces and the transitions to the crossguard and the butt in one process.

Mill the contour of the blade as well.

The blank is then smoothed all around with P240.

5.3 Working Out the Blade

Grind the surfaces of the guard and the back of the hilt on a flat surface. The transitions to the protective inlays should no longer show any edges. Then mark the centerline of the blade on the underside of the blank. This marked line serves as a guide point when we work with the belt sander.

Grind the transitions from the hilt to the inlays on a flat surface.

Place the blank on a plane surface and mark the blade's centerline with the height marker.

We mark the end of the blade contour on both sides with a marker. Matching our pattern, we also draw in the upper grinding line. To work systematically, we fit the blank properly into the vise and mark along each of the jaws.

To make symmetrical markings, we put the blade in the vise and mark the end of the blade contour.

We mark the height of the line. Matching the pattern, the height line runs parallel to the blade exactly to the point.

Mark the height line on both sides of the vise jaws.

Work toward the tip on the flat grinding device of the belt sander, orienting on the centerline of the blade and the ricasso. Start the job with a hard paper (P60), but do not grind all the way to the ricasso. Since the belt does not go around the edge of the grinding device, a straight edge, not a radius, would result.

On the belt sander we work out the line (flat wedge cut) step by step. At the tip of the blade we bring the cut upward. It is important to make sure to work up to the marked edges as exactly as we can when grinding.

Work evenly on both sides to avoid possible tensions in the steel from warping during hardening.

The blade thickness is ground out (some 0.015" [0.4 mm]). Now we work on the upper edge of the blade, strengthening the pressure to the edge.

Smooth the blade with a finer belt (P150). To keep a radius in the transition to the ricasso, we let the band overhang a bit, so that it can curve around the flat grinding direction.

The state of our blank after the work on the belt sander.

After working with the belt sander, we polish the blade with P240 paper. An attaching aid (see picture) prevents the surfaces from being scratched. Alternatively, the blade can be placed naturally in the vise, in which case the blank should be protected properly (pad jaws with aluminum or wood).

To be able to work out the upper edge of the blade, we must thin the blade appropriately on the upper side. With a marker, draw in the edge on each side of the blade and extend these lines to the tip. Along this edge we thin the front part of the blade on both sides. Here we work crudely with a file and then smooth it fine with P240. We always smooth in the direction of the blade tip.

Smooth the blade lengthwise with P240 sandpaper and a sanding block.

Re-mark the height line.

To maintain a straight line all the way, thin the front part of the blade where we have already raised the blade cutting. Work along the height line with a file.

Work alternately on the edge and surface with P240 and a hard sanding block until we form a precise height line.

Next we mark the facet on the upper side of the blade. For this we draw a line extending the back of the blade to the tip. The middle of the blade is marked on the upper side. The facet is filed and finally smoothed with a sanding block and P240/ P400 paper, always in the direction of the tip. Here too, we make sure to work exactly along the markings to create cleanly contoured edges.

The lower edge of the false edge is formed. It extends the line of the back to the tip of the blade.

Mark the centerline with the height marker.

File the false edge.

Then smooth the filed area with P240.

5.4 Working on the Hilt Contour and Lanyard Eye

On the wire-eroded knife, we also work out the lanyard eye along with the hilt contour. In later steps we satinize the handle and polish the scales. Here it is helpful to have a free surface, so that we can work up to the edges without touching the adjoining finish.

Thus we mill grooves in the blank at the transition between the handle inlays and the knife. To test the layout and dimensions of the grooves, we first use our protective inlays for testing. When all is arranged correctly, we mill the grooves into the blank. Note the coordinates and our way of making them, so as to make both sides symmetrical.

To make sure that the groove runs parallel to the scale to bolster transition, make a test milling in the scale.

When everything is right, mill the groove in the blank.

Work out the grooves at the rear transition similarly.

Angle the edges on the underside of the hilt with a shaft miller. Here we make sure not to damage the transitions to the finger guard and the butt of the hilt. We will work out this area later by hand with sandpaper.

The lanyard eye is also milled in this work step. We mount the knife so that the milling radius runs parallel to the outer edge of the hilt. Work out the eye with the shaft miller.

To work out the lower edge, mount the shaft miller at a 20-degree angle.

Finish the lanyard eye on the round milling table. We set up the blank so that the eye can be milled parallel to the outer edge of the hilt.

Neatly grind the lanyard eye with a file and sandpaper up to P600. The other surfaces, including the blade, taperings, and transitions are also smoothed with P600. Remove the aluminum protective inlays. The knife is ready for hardening.

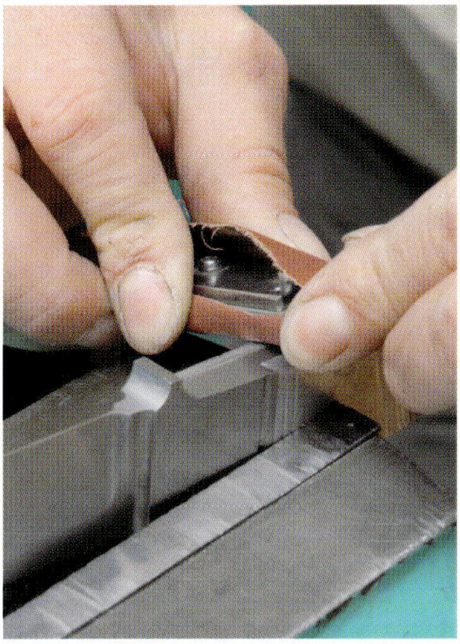

Smooth all the surfaces in steps from P240 to P400 to P600.

The area of the crossguard was also slimmed on the sides with a radius miller and then polished evenly with the underside of the hilt. At the rear of the hilt, file down the milled area by hand and let it run out to the butt.

With careful hammer blows, remove the protective handle inserts. Remove the adhesive residue. Our blank is now ready for heat treatment.

5.5 After Hardening

First check the hardened blank for warping. Then fit the handle material. For this particular project, this is problematic because of the shape and the meteorite material used. The meteorite stone is partly as hard as glass, but also includes other components such as nickel. Thus there is a danger of the material breaking when being worked—which should be avoided, what with the price of meteorites. Similar to working with semiprecious stones (lapis-lazuli, malachite), we use diamond tools—and a good deal of patience—to fit it.

Separate the meteorite material into the desired sizes. Grind the back flat and fit the height to the pockets of the knife. The contour of the protective inlays is transferred to the meteorite material and the silver plate inlays. The silver plates are fitted into the pockets and fixed with super glue. We make sure the surfaces are even and the fit is tight.

For the scales we prepare meteorite material and silver plate. The undersides of the meteorite scales have been ground flat. The fittings are done by hand with pattern aids.

The silver plates and the meteorite are set in place.

The meteorite pieces are now set in place. We check the fit very precisely with a magnifying glass. The scales are then set with super glue. Cut the scales carefully along the knife contour with a diamond cutting blade. Here we let some material project. Work the scales carefully with file and sandpaper until they are flush with the handle contour.

Check the fit of the scales under a stereo microscope.

Affix the inlays with super glue.

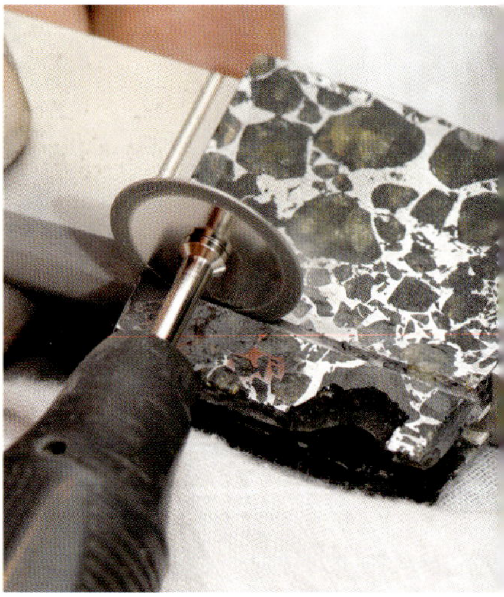

Remove the excess material with a diamond cutting blade.

Grind down the contours all around as carefully as possible.

Continue working out the contour with file and sandpaper.

5.6 Finishing

The knife is completely smoothed and satinized up to P1000 on all matte surfaces. The top and bottom are smoothed with P2000 and then polished with paste.

Using the same method as with the filed knife, a logo and other motifs are etched on the blade and hilt. Then the knife is sharpened and polished again. Finished!

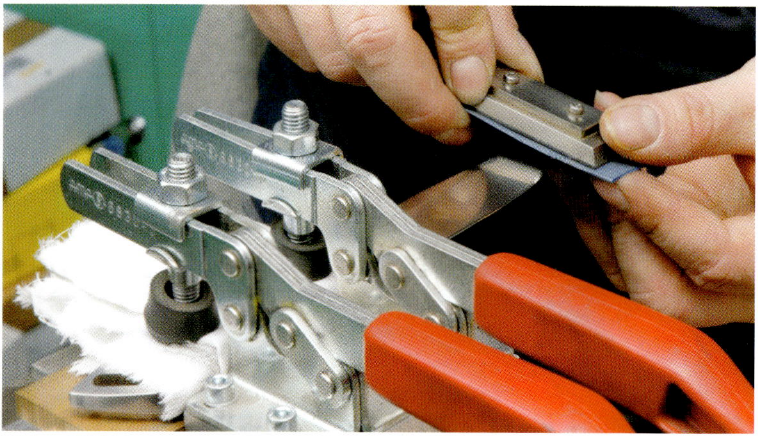

We smooth the blade and all surfaces up to P1000.

The etched logos are applied one after another.

Sharpen the blade with a diamond file.

Our finished integral knife with meteorite scales (Seymchan). The engravings show the motif from the plates of the Pioneer 10 and Pioneer 11 space ships—humanity's greeting to extraterrestrial life forms.

Basic Knife Making:
From Raw Steel to a Finished Stub Tang Knife.
Ernst G. Siebeneicher-Hellwig and Jürgen Rosinski.
In this book Ernst G. Siebeneicher-Hellwig and Jürgen Rosinski show the simplest and least expensive ways to construct a simple forge, make all necessary tools yourself, forge a stub tang blade from an old automobile coil spring, and make a complete knife.

Their practical guide demonstrates the most important theoretical basics and shows how simple it can be to experience bladesmithing. Each step is presented in text and pictures, with a special focus on forging the blade. Clear lists of tools and materials help you through the process. Practical tips, explanations of terms, and sketches round out the volume.

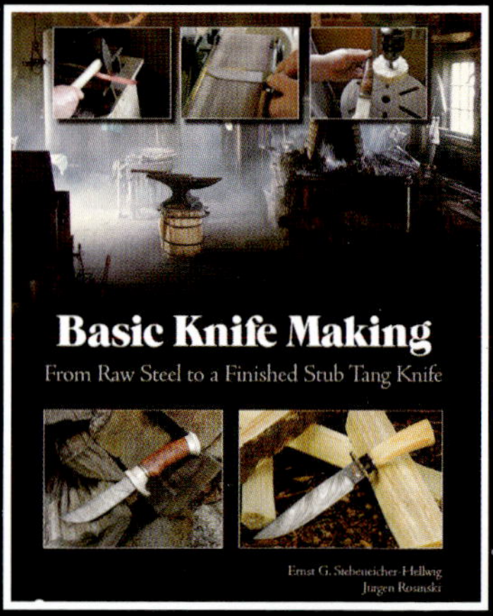

Size: 8 1/2" x 11" • 205 color images/10 drawings • 112 pp.
ISBN: 978-0-7643-3508-2 • soft cover • $29.99

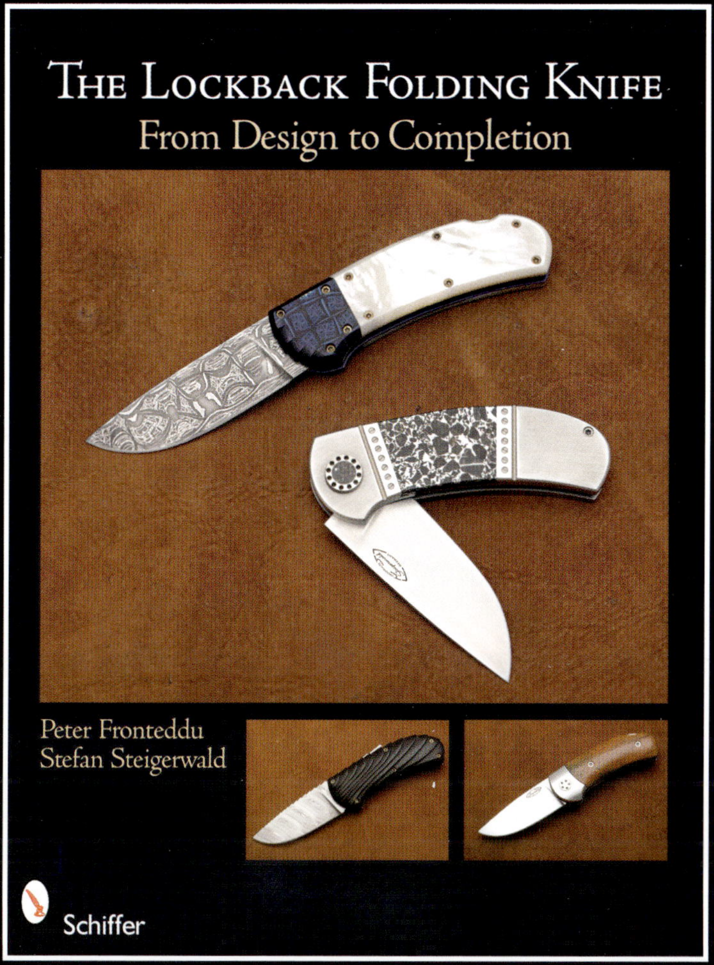
THE LOCKBACK FOLDING KNIFE
From Design to Completion
Peter Fronteddu
Stefan Steigerwald
Schiffer

Pocketknife Making for Beginners.
Stefan Steigerwald & Peter Fronteddu.
Make your own folding pocketknife with this easy-to-follow guide. Step by step, this instructional manual unfolds the secrets of constructing a slip-joint folding knife, which is held open by spring force and friction. In addition to introducing different variations of this knife style, this guide presents the materials, tools, and technical design skills needed for the project. Diagrams clearly demonstrate the mechanics of your knife and the crucial elements needed to make a properly functioning pocketknife. Detailed step-by-step explanations move from template to finished knife — even beginners can master this project with minimal tool requirements. Once the knife project is complete, you can use the processes in this guide and your own creativity to construct a special knife of your own design.

Size: 6" x 9" • 275+ photos & diagrams • 128 pp.
ISBN: 978-0-7643-3847-2 • spiral bound • $29.99